Mr. Yee  Fixes Cars

written by
ALICE K. FLANAGAN

photographs by
ROMIE FLANAGAN

Reading Consultant
LINDA CORNWELL
Learning Resource Consultant
Indiana Department of Education

CHILDREN'S PRESS®   *A Division of Grolier Publishing*
New York • London • Hong Kong • Sydney • Danbury, Connecticut

*Special thanks to Mike Yee
for allowing us to tell his story.*

*Also, thanks to Shellie, Jeff, Don, Gary,
Al, and especially Al's wife Kathy, who
made it all possible.*

Library of Congress Cataloging-in-Publication Data
Flanagan, Alice.
    Mr. Yee fixes cars / written by Alice K. Flanagan ; photographs by
Romie Flanagan ; reading consultant, Linda Cornwell.
       p.   cm. — (Our neighborhood)
    Summary: Follows an auto mechanic as he checks cars, finds out what
is wrong with them, and fixes the problems.
    ISBN 0-516-20772-5 (lib.bdg)   0-516-26297-1 (pbk.)
    1. Automobiles—Maintenance and repair—Juvenile literature.
[1. Automobiles—Maintenance and repair. 2. Occupations.] I. Flanagan,
Romie, ill. II. Title. III. Series: Our neighborhood (New York, N.Y.)
    TL147.F556   1998
    629.28'72—dc21
                             97-11863
                                CIP
                                AC

Photographs ©: Romie Flanagan

Hear a rattle in the engine?
Feel the steering wheel pull?

Bring the
problem to
Mr. Yee!

He fixes cars and can find out what's wrong. He's an auto mechanic.

At the beginning of his work day,
Mr. Yee checks the computer.

It shows him what the customer
wants fixed.

If the customer isn't sure what needs fixing, Mr. Yee must figure it out.

First, he listens for sounds that shouldn't be there—such as a knock, or a ping, or a strange burst of air.

Sometimes, he gets help from another mechanic.

Often, Mr. Yee puts the car up on a rack.

He looks underneath for parts that are worn out.

When Mr. Yee finds a problem, he writes down a list of what needs repair.

He shows the list to a service manager. The manager will get the customer's permission to let Mr. Yee work on the car.

Sometimes, Mr. Yee replaces parts on a car . . .

. . . the muffler,

the tires,

maybe even the brakes.

Usually, he changes the oil . . .

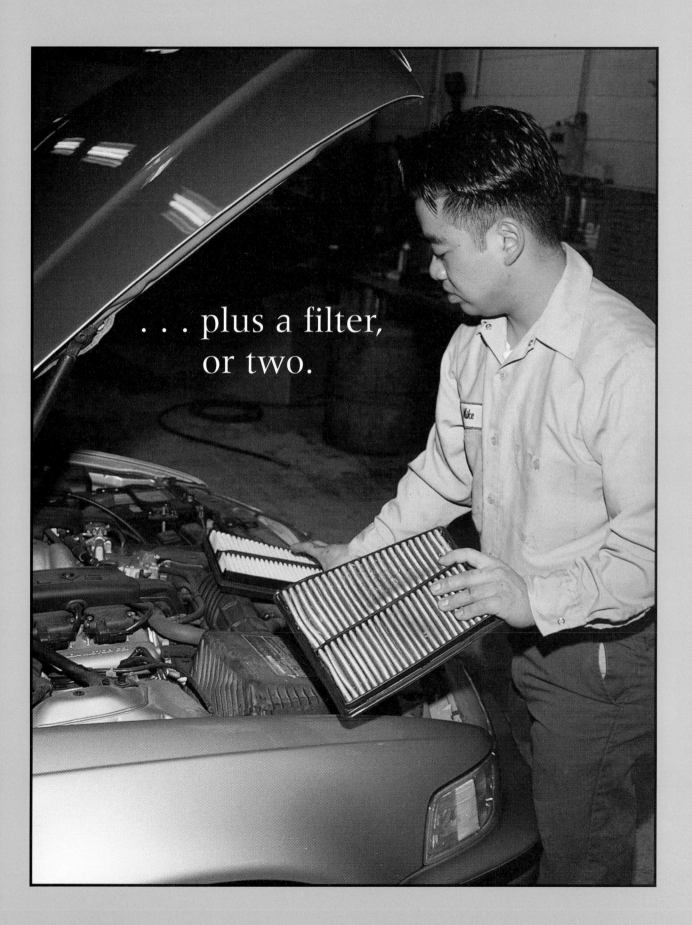

. . . plus a filter,
or two.

He may straighten the tires so the car will run smoothly.

If something goes wrong with the electrical parts, Mr. Yee gives the car a tune-up.

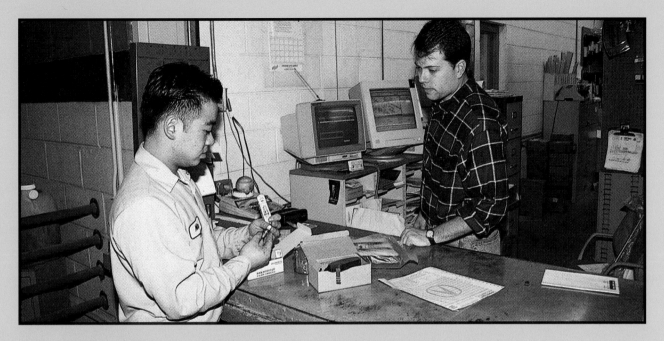

He puts in new spark plugs

and checks the battery.

If the problem is big, Mr. Yee might take the engine apart.

After Mr. Yee fixes the car, he writes down what he fixed and how much time the job took him to do.

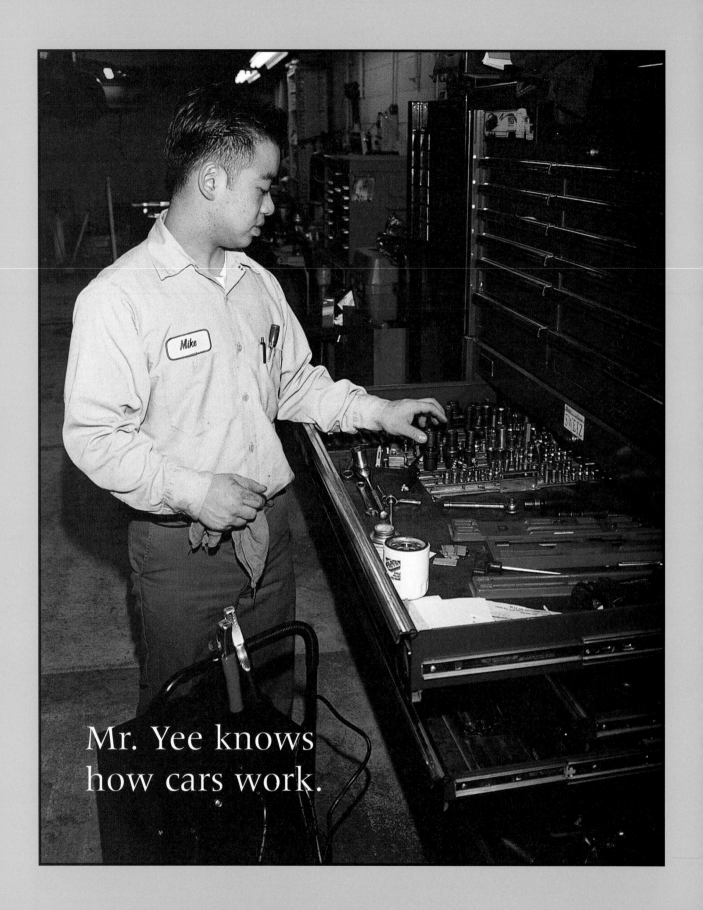

Mr. Yee knows how cars work.

He knows how to use hundreds
of different tools on thousands of
different car parts.

He has been fixing cars ever since he was a little boy. His father taught him how. As a teenager, Mr. Yee fixed cars as a hobby.

Mr. Yee went to a special school to learn about cars. Now he knows how to take them apart

and put them back together again!

Mr. Yee is proud of the work he does. He works on every car as if it were his own.

Meet the Author
and the Photographer

Alice and Romie Flanagan live in Chicago, Illinois, and have been involved in bookmaking for many years. Alice is a writer, and Romie is a photographer. As husband and wife, they enjoy working together closely. They hope their books help children learn about the people in their community and how their jobs affect their neighborhood.